CHASIN
HORIZONS

A POETIC JOURNEY THROUGH
THE MIND

A.J McGinty

DEDICATION

To my dear mum Isabella, who sadly passed away in *2021*, also my father Thomas whom I never got the chance to meet, and who passed in *1992*.

To my husband Jerry, my soulmate and best friend, to my daughters Sherri, Chantelle & Sinead, my grandson Damien & my granddaughters Hayleigh and Hannah.

Never have I been so happy or felt so much pride as I do now for my family, our bond can never be broken.

TABLE OF CONTENTS

PREFACE

Chasing Horizons is the third book of poetry I have written since *2015*, my first book of poetry named 'Tears On My Pillow' was more my life story through poetry, and in a sense a healing mechanism.

This new book of poetry is mainly about my thoughts through travel and time spent taking photos of the things that matter in life. It has taken around a year to finish and includes poetry I have written for others, some in memory of the children born into mother and baby homes.

INTRODUCTION

Enjoy the tender verses of this evocative collection as you journey with the poet as she looks deep into her soul, where each word is a brushstroke on the canvas of existence.

Chasing Horizons, invites you to explore the uncharted territories of emotion, love, loss and hope.

Through the delicate interplay of words the poet captures the essence of life's profound moments like a sailor charting his ship through the vast ocean of human experience.

With each poem, you will find yourself on a voyage chasing the ever elusive horizons that beckon in the distance.

Her poems form the gentle sequence of notes of natures rhythms to the thumping tumultuous storms of the heart, these verses resonate with the universal echoes of the human mind.

Join the poet on her journey of self-discovery, where every page is a step closer to the horizon we all pursue.

Chasing Horizons, is a poetic odyssey that will touch your heart and inspire your soul.

It's a timeless exploration of the beauty and the complexity of life, reminding us that, no matter where we are, we are all in pursuit of our own horizons.

ROAR OF THUNDER

A mid the cloak of night a sound that roars,
A symphony of rain, a thunderous score,
The heavens seep and tears cascade,
Upon the earth where shadows fade.

Every drop a whisper a secret shared,
A dance of water in the air ensnared,
It drops on the rooftop like a whispered plea,
A nocturnal waltz wild and free.

Flashes of lightening a fleeting sight,
Showing the world in an electric light,
The darkness parts just by a glance,
At the rain soaked world in a cosmic dance.

Windows rattle and trees bow low,
As the storms grand performance continues to grow,
Nature's fury and beauty unite,
This symphony is an awe inspiring night,

So let the raindrops serenade,
As thunder and lightening cascade,
In the velvet night of the nocturnal hour,
We find solace in nature's power.

WHISPERED SECRETS

In the forest glade where time stands still,
Stands the trees with branches crooked and surreal,
Beneath the sun's embrace they weave their tales,
Of whispers carried in the breeze of stories to unveil.

Crooked branches reaching out like hands,
Etching tales in bark like ancient mystic brands,
They have witnessed the seasons a timeless parade,
And cradled countless dreams in their quiet shade.

The stories they could tell if only we could hear,
Of loves tender moments and moments of fear,
A tapestry woven with threads of joy and sorrow,
Each crook and twist carrying hopes of tomorrow.

A couples laughter as they carve their names,
An old man's wisdom shared in evening flames,
The trees stand as a sentinel through life's sweet dance,
Its branches a canvas for memories to enhance.

Thunderous storms and raindrops they have weathered them all,
They stood resolute never to let life's tempests fall,
Whispering secrets to the moon on a clear starlit night,
Guiding lost souls with their mystical light.

Those crooked branches of the ancient trees,
They are keepers of tales as far as the eye can see,
Take a moment and listen when the wind softly blows,
For within these weathered limbs history enthralls.

ROYAL KIN

In ancient lands where thistles sway,
Through mist-kissed glens where legends play,
A heritage of royal blood I claim,
A Scottish heart aflame with pride, my name.

From highland shores to lowland plains,
A tapestry of history ingrained,
Brave ancestors fierce and free,
Their valors course deep within me.

The tartan's weave a sacred thread,
Binds me to the past where I tread,
Upon rugged moors and castles grand,
I stand as heir to this fine land.

Caledonia's Mountain high,
Beneath the azure of this Scottish sky,
I feel the echoes of the past,
A legacy of strength unsurpassed

So let the bagpipes plaintive cry,
Resound beneath the Northern sky,
For I am of Scottish royal kin,
A proud descendant, heart and soul within

SCOTLAND'S LAND MY HEARTS ABODE

A midst the highlands rugged grace,
Where ancient tales a whispered trace,
I find my heart forever bound,
To Scottish land where dreams are found.

The heather hills and purple sea,
Stretching to meet the endless sky,
Majestic Mountains touch the clouds,
Their lofty peaks where eagles fly.

Lochs that mirror nature's art,
Reflecting castles strong and grand,
A tapestry of history woven,
In this cherished Scottish land.

Scotland land of bracing breeze,
Your moors forever call,
With every crest and crag I roam.
A land unbreakable thats my home.

From Edinburgh's rickety street's,
To Glasgow's bustling beat,
I'm captivated by your charm,
In all the corners of every street

In love I stand forever true,
To your landscapes wild and free,
Scotland's land my hearts abode,
You are the home that sets me free.

WATERS EDGE

A t the waters edge I sit a soul at ease,
Listening to waves smash the rocks, a soothing breeze,
Thoughts like gentle ripples soft and slow,
In quiet tranquility they lovingly flow.

Seagulls dance in the salty breeze,
A symphony of nature a harmonious tease,
As the horizons embrace the setting sun,
I find myself in a moment of peace well spun.

Love and dreams intertwine with the lull of the sea,
A tapestry woven in whispers just for me,
With every tender drop of the water's kiss,
I'm reminded of life's beauty and its eternal bliss.

I remain by the waters gentle song,
Lost in a melody where I truly belong,
With thoughts as companions like dear friends they say,
In this moment of stillness on such a peaceful day

CHASING HORIZONS

In the realms of light where moments dance,
My amateur lens I take a chance,
Through viewfinders eye I seek to find,
The worlds beauty in frames defined.

My humble hand and shutter's grace,
I capture time with a fleeting embrace,
No mystery yet but a heart thats keen,
In every snapshot a story unseen

Sunrise and shadows long,
In whispered clicks I belong,
My novice journey and visual quest,
To freeze emotions at my best.

Through City streets or nature's door,
I click and wonder craving more,
Each frame a canvas raw and true,
Painting life's palette just for you

Framing smiles framing tears,
Moments stitched through the years,
Through amateur's grasp my spirit is free,
To seize the world as I see.

Imperfect shots I hold them dear,
For thats my steps year after year,
A photographic voyage all so sweet,
An amateur's heart with passion to complete.

VOICES

Those voices you heard inside your head,
　　Were cries of children waiting to be heard,
　　Beneath the earth is where we lay,
All this time from that fateful day.

Discarded like trash not a care in the world,
Cold hearts they had, were we that troubled?
Our mothers heartbroken they were,
The pain they suffered too much to bare.

They said, they were unaware,
Now you tell me how is that fair?
Is it enough just to say a prayer?
Our families hearts they cannot repair.

They turned a blind eye that you can be sure,
That blind eye they cannot restore,
They should hang their heads in shame,
They all must share the blame.

Where was their faith, where was their love?
Too soon they sent us to heaven above,
God did not want it this way,
It was their rules that took us that day.

So now we have been found we ask of you this,
Admit your sins and take us from this darkness,
Let our families heartbreak cease,
Only then will we rest in peace.

Written in 2017,
Sean Ross Abbey Commemorations in Roscrea, Tipperary. Ireland

SEAN ROSS ABBEY

LIFE'S IRONY

In the pursuit of happiness we look for success,
Chasing our dreams sometimes causing distress,
Life is a rollercoaster we must learn to smile,
Even only for a while.

The coffee spills, the bus is late,
Going to the dentist we got the wrong date,
We stumble we fumble yet we find a way,
Just smile we have another day.

HUMANITY

From distant lands we hear their cries,
Through endless struggles they endure,
Where there is darkness, we should bring light,
Like a torch shinning through the night.

Let us not forget our humble start,
From birth we are connected at heart,
We breath the same air under one sun,
A journey together as one

We should cherish this gift, this chance,
Together we stand in life's grand dance,
We are travellers on this moral plain,
Let compassion our legacy, let love remain.

FINDING OUR WAY

Education is a precious key,
Unlocking our minds to possibility,
A beacon of light through a world so vast,
Igniting the fire of knowledge to last.

In letters and numbers we'll find our way,
Building the foundations day by day,
Times tables and grammar rules,
We navigate through what education fuels.

Through art and music we express our hearts,
And discover the beauty of various arts,
Through science and experiments we unravel,
The mysteries of life for which we travel.

Education has the power to transform,
It lifts us and makes us perform,
Education is a beacon of light,
Guiding all through day and night

May we always strive to expand our minds,
For knowledge is a treasure that eternally binds,
Building moral values shaping our souls,
Giving most empathy and plugging the holes

OVER THE POND

U pon Scottish shores I took my first breath,
A land of highlands and glens life's grand quest,
Beneath the sky's tartan I learned to explore,
In misty moors and castles galore.

But destiny whispered a tale untold,
Across the Irish seas my heart was cajoled,
My roots I must journey to lands draped in green,
Where legends and laughter forever convene

From my home street to Ireland's embrace,
I sailed the waves seeking my place,
A bridge of connection Cross Celtic expanse,
Where Scotland and Ireland share song and dance.

The bagpipes lament met the fiddlers sweet croon,
A harmony woven in sun and in moon,
In glens and in valleys united they stand,
My birth and my roots go hand in hand.

From haggis to Irish stew a culinary delight,
I tasted the flavours of both day and night,
The highlands and cliffs of Moher so wide,
Two homelands together side by side.

Though borders may part them on maps they design,
In my hearts compass their spirits entwine,
Scotland and Ireland a tale to be told,
My birth and my roots forever I'll hold.

FAMILY

In the garden of my heart it blooms so bright,
A families love and endless light,
My husband, anchor of my life's grand sea,
With daughters three, a bond forever free.

In you my love I found my dearest friend,
Through every twist and turn until the end,
With every sunrise and each setting sun,
Our love has grown a journey that's begun.

Our girls are stars that light my darkest night,
With grace and strength they shine with pure delight,
Each one a treasure a unique embrace,
Together we find joy in every space.

Two granddaughters like flowers in full bloom,
With innocence and beauty that consumes.
Their laughter dances through the sweetest air,
A testament to a love beyond compare.

With love that flows like the river to the sea,
My family is my greatest symphony,
With husband, daughters, grandson and two,
My heart is filled with love for all of you.

For my husband, my daughters, my grandson and granddaughters

x

WHERE WATER FLOWS

Where water flows and grass grows love does bloom,
In natures dance it finds an ample room,
Through winding rivers it does glide,
In meadows green where beauty abides.

Like waters course love's path may twist and turn,
Yet in its journey we forever yearn,
It flows through life a constant gentle stream,
In every heart it's more than just a dream.

In meadows love's like grass soft and free,
It spreads its roots a vast and endless sea,
Though seasons change it stands the test of time,
In every verse in every subtle rhyme.

Though challenges may come like storms at sea,
Love's deep connection helps us to be free,
Where water flows and grass grows love is our song,
Enduring, eternal, and forever strong

FOREVER TRUE

In emerald lands where legends bloom,
Where rugged coasts kiss oceans plume,
Resides a spirit fierce and true,
My Irish roots a cherished view.

From ancient tales of warriors bold,
To music that warms my heart and soul,
A heritage of strength and grace,
My Irish roots a noble embrace.

Through rolling hills of green so grand,
A timeless beauty a native land,
A legacy of stories shared,
My Irish roots beyond compare.

With laughter that could light the stars,
And kindness that could heal all scars,
In every step and every vow,
My Irish roots, oh wow.

A history of legacy wide,
Where hope and courage coincide,
In every dance and every tune,
My Irish roots forever bloom.

I'll raise a glass to kin and clan,
To castles old and fields that span,
With love and pride I stand anew,
My Irish roots forever true.

MY RAGAMUFFINS

I n a world of boundless skies so blue,
Two souls arrived so pure and true,
With eyes like stars they stole my heart,
Two small dogs a work of art

Furry paws and wagging tails,
They dance through life leaving trails,
Of joy and laughter in their wake,
Two little hearts for goodness sake

Through mornings light and twilights grace,
They offer love in every embrace,
Their presence warms both day and night,
In their company worries sway.

The tales they tell with their boundless glee,
Running wild and forever free,
Yet in the stillness of the night,
They curl beside me a comforting sight.

In rain or sunshine we're a trio strong,
Sharing life's journey be it short or long,
Their love is fierce their spirit bright,
My two small dogs my guiding light.

With every bark and every play,
They weave their love in every way,
In their tiny frames courage takes its place,
And in their gaze I find solace and grace.

Here's to my companions forever dear,
In my heart you hold a treasure clear,
My two small dogs my joys untold,

CHASING HORIZONS

Forever and always my love you hold.

ROSIE & DAWSON

DREAMS & WONDERS

Upon wings of steel I take to the sky,
Bound for lands where dreams and wonders lie,
Above the clouds I find a tranquil throne,
A realm of thought where seeds of wonder are sown.

As the engines roar and the world falls away,
I'm suspended in time in a magical way,
Gazing through quilted clouds and blue seas,
My mind takes flight unburdened and free.

Thoughts like birds in graceful arcs do soar,
Exploring landscapes I've not seen before,
Musing life's journey with care,
A canvas of moments a masterpiece so rare

To a beautiful country my flight takes me,
But within a universe of thoughts roams free,
I am a traveller by air, land and sea,
In the embrace of wonder my soul sets free.

Let the wings of thought continue to soar,
As I journey within seeking treasures galore,
Deep in thought in the airplane's embrace,
I find a serenity a boundless space.

DEAR DAD

In the realms beyond where stars embrace the night,
Where love's eternal glow casts a gentle light,
My father dear, though never met in life.
Your spirit's presence soothes my heart's deep strife.

Though time's cruel hand did steal our chance to be,
Your love and care I never did see,
I feel your whispers in the breeze's sigh,
A guardian angel forever nigh

Through unseen threads a bond we share so true,
A love untouched by distance grew,
In dreams you visit, heart to heart we speak,
In every twinkling star your love is unique.

Though brief your time on earth did lay,
Your legacy of love will never sway,
You're not forgotten never will you fade,
In tender moments your essence stayed.

Father dear, though fate did set us apart,
You live within the chambers of my heart,
In heavens embrace where you now reside,
With love unending you and I are tied.

So here's to you a daughters prayer,
For in my heart there's always a chair,
Though we never met, your presence is clear,
My father in heaven forever near.

"In Memory of My Father Thomas Black McGinty 1935-1992"

27

GOODBYES ARE NOT FOREVER

God seen the tired look upon your face,
The day he took you home to rest,
Today is your final journey home,
Your final resting place, but you are not alone.

I'll think of you every day,
But that is nothing new,
Because I though of you yesterday,
And the days before that too

I will think of you in silence,
Every day I will speak your name,
Remember we have our memories,
And pictures of you in frames.

Your memory is my keepsake,
With which I will never part,
God has you in his keeping,
I have you in my heart.

My loving memories will never die,
As the years roll on and days pass by,
I will smell sweet scented roses,
As I look upon the sky.

Goodbyes are not forever,
Goodbyes are not the end,
It simply means I will miss you,
Until we meet again.

Now in the arms of angels,
You flew away from here,
I know you are in good hands,

I love and miss you dear.

"Written on the day of my mum's cremation"

GBNF

For those who have gone before me,
I think of you every day,
I know you walk beside me,
Like a gentle wisp of hay.

Sometimes a little cold spot,
Right behind my ear,
And a little tap on my shoulder,
You're telling me you're here.

You watch the tears roll down my cheeks,
Whilst my heart is beating fast,
Holding out your hand while telling me,
The pain you feel won't last.

I know that life goes on without you,
And the pain is hard to bear,
But knowing you walk beside me,
Shows how much you cared.

You are gone but not forgotten,
I know now I can survive,
Holding you're photo in my hand,
As I keep your memory alive.

AS I TALK TO YOU

Never in fifty-seven years have I heard your voice,
Yet I have a conversation with you every day,
Believe me when I say, it was not my choice,
Neither had I planned it this way.

At thirty-four I learned your name,
Until then I hadn't known you existed,
My mission was to find you,
I'm so glad I persisted.

With not much help from others,
I set out on my own,
Through anger I searched you calmly,
One by one picking up every stone.

Off to the records office to see the woman there,
I gave her your details and waited with baited breath,
What she told me next left me in despair,
 I was not prepared for death.

I set out to look for family perhaps there were a few?
I soon discovered cousins and three brothers too,
I carried on searching and found family across the pond,
Only then did I believe you waved your magic wand.

Some years later I had a message sent to me,
Should I call her, Wondering who could this be?
The woman said she was your daughter,
Now I have four siblings not just three.

MY NAME IS MCGINTY

My name is Mcginty a mother of three daughters I am,
Grew up in Scotland but my roots are of Irish land,
Many a trip I take over those Irish shores,
You'll know me when I come knocking your door.

If only I knew back then what I know now,
An effort I would have made somehow,
The Irish blood that runs through my veins,
My roots I would gladly have lain.

With family in both north and the south,
Some of whom took to the sea for want of a better life,
Australia, Canada US and more,
Too far away for me to knock on their door.

Family in Antrim, Donegal and Galway too,
A family going back hundreds of years, who knew,
DNA contact was all that I had,
Now I've met them face to face and I'm glad.

Stories to tell from family I've found,
Keeps my feet firmly on Irish ground,
Stories through music I love to hear,
Now things are becoming so clear.

Now knowing my roots I feel almost complete,
Only one thing missing I must keep him discreet,
Alive I must keep him in my heart and my head,
For without him one half of me would be dead.

So Ireland embrace me with your love,
Keep singing those songs I'm so proud of,

CHASING HORIZONS

I'll keep crossing those Irish shores,
You'll know me when I come knocking your door.

DADDY'S KISS

A fathers touch a daddy's kiss,
A grieving daughter,
Who had lots she missed,
An empty house and empty chair,
A father who was not there.

A broken heart a tearful eye,
I wasn't able to say goodbye,
Things I should have had,
When thinking of my dad

LISTEN

Listen to the birds in the trees,
The crickets over yonder,
And the silence of me

Listen to the crackle of the leaves,
Nothing in the sky except clouds,
As we talk as we breath.

Listen to your thoughts,
That only you can hear,
Not a word only a tear

Time will pass,
Life goes on,
Thoughts kept inside your head,
Only you can put to bed.

CRIES UNNOTICED

I did not want to go home so soon,
Listen up I was tuned to the moon,
I did not ask to be depressed,
It's an illness no less.

It could be finances, it could be death,
It really doesn't matter its grief non the less,
People deal with grief in all sorts of ways,
My mind, it was in a different place.

I cried out for help from those who could have helped,
But you plied me with pills, the side affects, they made me ill,

Those pills you gave me,
You said would make me better,
I followed the instructions right to the letter.

Everything was cloudy each and every day,
Those pills you gave me, they made it that way,
I couldn't think straight nor for myself,
Here I was left on the shelf.

My cries they went unnoticed,
You didn't listen, you didn't focus,
Time and money was your excuse,
You may as well have held the noose.

(Suicide Prevention)

THANK YOU

Whilst we had to say goodbye,
There is something you should know,
With broken hearts and no dry eye,
Our heartfelt thanks we must show.

For without your quick thinking,
Our girl we would have lost,
But that was only the beginning,
Because every bridge you crossed.

You were more than just a friend,
You saved a life too,
One out of two wasn't bad,
And that was because of you.

So when we said goodbye to you,
Know how much we cared,
We will think of you always,
And the joy that we shared.

(In Memory of Bobby Howard)

THE BABIES

Love was all we wanted,
In life and in death,
Who were you to take us,
From our mothers breast.

Those of us who made it,
Sold and sent to foreign shores,
The secrets that you kept,
Behind those closed doors.

Some of us had good lives,
And others not so much,
Still you kept your secret,
Everyone made to hush.

Now that we are older,
And we think of all the rest,
The one's you wrapped in cloth,
And lay beneath the earth.

No love did you show them,
No coffin for them to lay,
Thinking of your next dollar,
Then went about your day.

Now what about the mothers?
Those you looked down on,
You told them they were sinners,
Everything was just a con.

You caused so much damage,
With your preaching thats a fact,
Sometimes with a heavy hand,

And vicious tongue you attacked.

All we want is justice,
For the atrocities and YOUR sins,
Yet you still believe you done nothing,
You all have such thick skin.

We will not give up,
Not the survivors nor the rest,
We will keep on fighting,
You have caused so much distress.

You took away our identity,
You sold us to the rich,
To feed your filthy lives,
And all without a glitch

Now the doors have opened,
Your lies and sins exposed,
The world knows now,
The treatment you imposed.

For those who have gone before us,
We WILL see justice done,
It may take some time,
But justice, indeed will come.

(In support of the survivors of mother and baby homes around the world)

TINY FEET

You cannot hear the pitter patter,
For beneath the earth we lay,
The tiny feet that does matter,
Discarded like a lump of clay.

Cold, soggy and wet,
Wrapped in a piece of rag,
With all the children whom we met,
Not a care, not even a name tag.
Put inside a great big hole,
Hidden out of site,
They were the ones who had control,
No remorse, not in the slight

They say our mothers committed a sin,
And they had to pay the price,
They ignored the pain within,
Those nuns were cold as ice.

Darkness is all we have ever known,
Will we ever see some light?
For into the ground we were thrown,
On a dark and lonely night

We were butterflies and angels,
Waiting to take flight,
Our stories are not fables,
We are simply waiting to say goodnight.

So please continue to fight,
Do not be afraid to speak,
It is your god's given right,
To seek justice for the weak.

CHASING HORIZONS

(In memory of all the babies and children who passed too soon, and for their families who have the voice to shout it loud)

BREATHTAKING LANDSCAPES

In a world filled with vibrant colours and breathtaking landscapes there lived a young filmmaker called Michaela.

She had a unique ability to see beauty even in the most ordinary things, and her heart overflowed with an immense appreciation for the world around her.

Every morning Michaela would wake up with a sense of excitement, eager to explore the wonders that lay beyond her doorstep.

She lived in a cozy cottage nestled at the edge of a lush Forrest, where trees whispered secrets to the wind and the flowers bloomed in a riot of colours.

The birds serenaded her with melodious tunes, and the gentle babbling of a nearby brook provided a soothing soundtrack to her days.

One day she ventured deeper into the forest, she stumbled upon a hidden glade blanketed in a tapestry of wild flowers.

Their petals swayed in the breeze in a symphony of colours, and butterflies danced among them in a joyful celebration of life.

Michaela couldn't resist the urge to capture this enchanting scene, with each click of her camera, she infused the scene with the same sense of wonder that filled her heart.

As seasons changed, her explorations took her beyond the forest, leading her to vast meadows where the grass seemed to ripple like waves on the sea.

She marvelled at the grandeur of towering mountains that kissed the sky, their peaks often hidden beneath wisps of ethereal clouds.

She walked along serene beaches, where the sunset painted the horizon in hues of orange, pink and gold, leaving her breathless.

During her journey, Michaela encountered people from all walks of life, each with their own stories to tell.

Through their tales, she discovered that the worlds beauty not just in its landscapes, but also in the kindness and resilience of its inhabitants.

She saw the bonds of friendship that formed like delicate blossoms, and the way the community came together to support each other in times of need.

But it wasn't just the natural and human beauty that captivated her, she found artistry in the every day, the intricate patterns of a seashell, the mesmerising rhythm of raindrops on her window, and the laughter of people in the street.

She realised it was all waiting to be noticed and appreciated by those with open hearts and attentive eyes.

Michaela's work began to gain attention, and people from all corners of the world marvelled at her ability to capture the essence of beauty in her creations.

Through her filmmaking she shared her perspective, inspiring others to pause and see the world through fresh eyes.

Michaela's story serves as a reminder that the world is a breathtaking masterpiece, filled with wonders big and small, waiting for us to acknowledge and cherish it.

HILLS OF SCOTLAND

In a quiet village among the Pentland hills of Scotland, lived a woman named Lady Ann Jane. With eyes as blue as the skies above, and a heart as gentle as the highland winds, she was the embodiment of the proud Scottish spirit that had been passed down through generations of her royal heritage.

From a young age, Lady Ann Jane had been regaled with tales of her ancestors, who had once ruled these lands with wisdom and strength. The stories told of Kings and Queens who had donned tartan kilts and wielded broadswords, leading their clan with honour, and determination.

She felt an unbreakable bond with those legends, as if echoes of their courage still whispered through the glens. Every year villages held highland games, a celebration of Scottish culture and history.

Lady Ann Jane eagerly awaited this event, for it was a chance to honour her heritage in a tangible way. With a kilt of the clan's tartan proudly worn, she would participate in the caber toss, throwing a heavy log with strength that seemed to come from the very soul of her ancestors.

The crowd would cheer as the caber soared through the air, a symbol of resilience and determination. But her pride in her royal heritage extended beyond athletic feats she had inherited a love of Scottish music, and the haunting notes of bagpipes often filled the air as she practiced fervently.

The melodies seemed to carry the weight of the past, telling stories of battles fought and love lost. Inspiring a deep connection to the history that flowed through her veins.

As she grew older, the sense of pride in her heritage only intensified, she delved into genealogy, tracing her linage back to ancient Kings and Queens who's names were etched in history books.

Lady Ann Jane's room became a mini museum, adorned with plaques, portraits and other royal artefacts that paid homage to the legacy of her forebears. Yet, amidst the tales of glory and honour, she understood that her royal heritage was not without complexities. The stories spoke of struggles and sacrifices, of alliance forged and broken.

This awareness only deepened her appreciation for the resilience that had been passed down, a reminder that her pride wasn't just about basking in the glory of the past, but also about carrying the lessons and values forward into the future.

Lady Ann Jane walks the path of her linage, determined to make her mark in a way that would make those who came before her proud.

THE GOLDEN YEARS

One day, a group of young children gathered at my porch, gazing at the setting of the sun, one of the children asked, "What's the best thing about getting old?"

My eyes twinkled with a mixture of nostalgia and hope, I began to tell the children a story about my own life, a tale that spoke of beauty and joy that came with embracing the golden years.

I was much like all of you, full of energy and eager to explore the world around me, I had dreams and aspirations, and I worked hard to achieve them.

I have experienced the ups and downs life brings, but as the years went by, something magical happened. I began to realise that age wasn't a barrier, it was a gift.

I went on to share adventures in later years of how I had traveled to far off places I had only dreamt of, how I had taken up writing, and discovered a hidden talent and how I formed deep and lasting friendships with people at home and over the pond.

Getting old isn't about the number of years you have lived, its about the experiences you've gathered along the way, its about the wisdom that comes from weathering life's storms, and basking in its sunny days.

Every wrinkle on my face holds a memory, every grey hair tells a tale, and I wouldn't change any of it for the world.

As the children listened intently, my story inspired them to see ageing in a new light. They began to understand that growing older meant growing wiser and richer in experiences, knowledge and love.

As the years rolled by, I told them to cherish every moment, knowing that every passing day brought them closer to a future filled with endless possibilities.

As we get older, children learn from us elders while we elders learn from the children.

JOAN

You were a gift,
Wrapped with love,
That will continue to shine,
From heaven above

Those who knew you,
Will know what I mean,
Love, compassion everything in between,
You were someone whom everyone could lean.

God called you home,
He needs you now,
Mother to all angels,
Who will gladly take a bow.

Into his loving arms,
The best teacher for sure,
So many will look up to you,
Like so many before.

With heavy heart,
I say not goodbye,
Your wise words will live with me,
Until the day I die.

Save me a place,
I'll take it gladly,
With love and with grace.

(In loving memory of Joan Coghill" April 2018)

JOAN

MOTHER DEAREST

In memory of my mother so gentle and kind,
With love and warmth forever in my heart I'll find,
A beautiful soul with a heart so pure,
In my memories your love will always endure.

With eyes that sparkled like stars in the night,
You brought love and comfort with your loving light,
You're smile a beacon in my darkest hours,
Guiding me with grace like the springtime flowers.

Though you've left this world and tears often fall,
You're spirit lives on in me in the memories I recall,
In every sunrise in every breeze that sighs,
I sense your presence like you're in the skies.

Your legacy of love like the river that flows,
Through generations will steadily grow,
You were the heart and soul of my family tree,
Forever in my heart you'll be.

In quiet moments when I feel you near,
I'll remember your love so strong and sincere,
Though you've left this world your love will never depart,
For you will continue to live on in my grateful heart.

Here's to you mum with love so true,
In my memories I'll forever cherish you,
A beautiful woman with a heart so warm,
In my heart you'll forever be the calm to my storm.

In Loving Memory of My Mum Isabella Johnston McKinlay Bird
1942-2021

MUM

FATHER'S DAY

It's father's day again,
My thoughts turn to you,
Wishing you were here with me,
But then, what could I do?

They didn't tell me you existed,
Until it was too late,
Now every father's day,
My heart will always ache.

I have your picture in my hand,
Trying to imagine,
The life we could have had,
If they had taken action

They say that the eyes,
Are the window to the soul,
If you could see inside mine now,
My heart you could console.

So with heavy heart,
I listen to my song,
And say my prayer to God,
Please don't make this day too long.

(In Loving Memory of My Father 1935-1992)

DAD

ANTHEMS OF FREEDOM

In melodies that rise & fall,
In lyrics that embrace the soul,
A universal chorus calls,
A tune where hearts are whole.

For every line that's softly sung,
A mirror of our joys and fears,
In every note, a thread is strung,
Connecting us through passing years

The ballads of love, so pure and true,
Resonate in every beating heart,
For who hasn't felt affection's hue,
And danced in enchanting art.

In verses that speak of trials endured,
We find our battles, our inner strife,
The strength we seek, the hope assured,
In rhythms that guide us through life.

In tunes that share of loss and pain,
Each tear we shed each scar we wear,
We find out stories aren't in vain,
In melodies that deeply care.

From every corner of the earth,
In different tongues, in varied ways,
Through songs we're granted rebirth,
A unity that forever stays.

So let us cherish these harmonies,
These verses that make us feel alive,
In lyrics we find our own stories,

CHASING HORIZONS

A tapestry of how we survive,

No matter where our journey starts,
Or what our days on earth may bring,
In songs, we're joined heart to heart,
Together in the song we all can sing

HAND IN HAND

If you could take my hand,
No matter in wake or sleep,
I know I would hold you tight,
You would be mine to keep.

Not one day goes by,
Without you on my mind,
Your heart and mine,
Will always be entwined.

Although I never met you,
Nor had you in my life,
Trust me when I whisper,
It cut me like a knife.

The more I hear about you,
Which often makes me smile,
Especially now I know,
You knew me all the while.

I understand that things were hard,
Wishing you could be with me,
There were things that got in the way,
And even people that kept you at bay.

There were obstacles that kept us apart,
But in distance you kept me in your heart,
If I knew back then what I know now,
I would have been with you somehow.

So here me, I love you very much,
I longed to be in your clutch,
Like a glider just waiting to land,

But only when hand in hand.

DAYS GONE BY

Were did those days go,
When we played kick the can,
They were such happy times.
While waiting for the rag man.

Running around not a care in the world,
Playing skipping ropes feeling so thrilled,
Hide and seek was so much fun,
While the boys played with toy guns.

Cowboys and Indians was their thing,
While the girls settled on swings,
We played shop and built a den,
And the grown up's they called us hen.

We played doctors and nurses, what did we know,
In reality we had a crush on them beau's
We played a game called Chucky,
Sometimes with money if we were lucky.

We would hear the rag man shout "Any old rags"
Then we'd go running looking for bags,
We'd poke a hole in an old jumper.
Then hear our mums shout, "I'm going to thump her"

So many games we played back then,
Lots of fresh air while kicking that can,
Now there is technology what a whack,
I think it's time we brought it all back.

AUTUMN LEAVES

In the autumn's gentle breeze a breeze so cool,
Through misty fog they weave a tranquil rule,
Whispering secrets they dance with grace,
Caressing the world in a beautiful space.

Those leaves once vibrant now adorn the ground,
An array of colours nature's art profound,
With every step they rustle and sigh,
Like bidding farewell as the seasons fly.

The fog like a veil wraps the world in a haze,
Adding some mystery to those autumn days,
They mingle with the breeze like acting a scene,
Where reality and dreams entwine so serene.

Together they create a colourful sights,
With a dance of pure delights,
Embrace the autumn my friends,
For in its beauty a story it sends.

A CASTLE TALE

In the depth of the castle a tale is told,
Where spirits roam and stories unfold,
In the dark of night and whispers abound,
A feeling of cold and eerie sounds.

Within those ancient halls of stone,
A presence is sorrowfully unknown,
Where memories linger trapped in time's embrace,
The castle's ghosts leave their trace.

Amidst the walls of the mourning grey,
A lady weeps long gone astray,
Her heart broken from an untimely death,
Her ethereal form she was never blessed.

In a dim-lit corridor her love's armour gleams,
His spirit cries burdened by shattered dreams,
Betrayed by a king in perpetual despair,
Often wondering through the midnight air.

From castle to castle ghosts drift and glide,
Their translucent figures and secrets they hide,
A whispered echo through stained glass,
Telling stories of tragedy from their distant past

Some find peace in the castle's charm,
While others fearing spectral harm,
Those ghostly residents still yearning release,
Look for those who will listen and provide them peace.

If you dare to venture through a castles door,
Be prepared for ghosts never seen before,
For in the shadows their stories come alive.

Like bee's disturbed from their hive.

WINTER SNOW

In the chill of a cold winters night when skies turn grey,
A wonderland emerges ice, snow and fey,
There's a silence in snowflakes falling all pure and white,
An enchanting tranquility in the dark of night

With every breath a mist of clouds escapes the air,
As stars twinkle in a magical flare,
My garden dressed in a white gown pristine and new,
My camera in hand at the captivating view.

From trees and branches snowflakes slowly descend,
Softly landing in a graceful blend,
A blanket on the ground in a coat of pure white,
A beautiful sight under the sky's soft light.

Cold winter nights hold secrets and tales,
Of mystic creatures hidden in snowy trails,
As winter's touch freezes in time gentle and still,
Brings a moment of tranquility and dreams have their fill.

So lets enjoy this winters wonderful embrace,
Admiring the beauty that cold cannot erase,
In these quiet moments warmth can be found,
In such a calm cold winter night where peace is profound.

THIS CHRISTMAS

This Christmas like any other,
I think of you my dear mother,
You may be gone from my sight,
But your with me each and every night

In my dreams and in my heart,
That alone can't keep us apart,
I still hear your laugh and see your smile,
Even if only once in a while.

The little Robin you sent last year,
Sat on my fence ever so dear,
I got the message it sent to me,
Before it flew back to thee.

So this Christmas like every other,
I feel your presence my dear mother,
I smell your scent I know you are here,
Never gone, always near.

ACKNOWLEDGMENTS

Sinead for being my listening ear when I've read back poems for this Chasing Horizons

My readers, for purchasing copies of my books and their very kind reviews for which I am always grateful.

The many friends I have made along the way, be it from purchasing my books, on my travels attending commemorations/memorials, you will always have a place in my heart.

A.J McGinty

ABOUT THE AUTHOR

Since childhood A.J's passion was to one day write at least one book, fast forward to *2015*, when she published her first book 'Sad, Lonely & A Long Way from Home'. She has since gone on to publish several more, not only has she continued to write, she is also an advocate and supporter of the survivors of Religiously Run Institutions, which had led her on the path to investigative journalism.

A.J has also gone on to study has and gained certificates in: forensic psychology, and investigating psychology and human rights & law.

Now that this, Chasing Horizons has been published, she has begun writing a heptalogy series of books with the first called **'House of Annie Linn Bird.'**

As these are a heptalogy series they will be short stories apposed to full length novels.

A.J hopes to also publish next year *2024* the second part of 'The Empty Swing' Which originally wasn't planned, however, after many requests for a part two she thought it was only right that her readers got to know about, life after Lily.

A.J is also an amateur photographer and frequently travels, she has also been working on a new project which she hopes to fulfil between *2024/26*, her very own 'My DNA Journey' Which will begin in Norway and take her to the Orkney Isles, Ireland then finishing back in Scotland.

Follow A.J on Twitter: https://www.twitter.com/AJMcGinty56
Instagram: AJMcginty56
Website: www.ajmcginty56.co.uk

OTHER BOOKS BY THIS AUTHOR

Under the pseudonym: Belinda Conniss

SECRETS TO THE GRAVE (Non-Fiction)
BEHIND CLOSED DOORS (Non-Fiction)
THE EMPTY SWING (Fiction)
TEARS ON MY PILLOW (Poetry)
WHERE WATER FLOWS AND GRASS GROWS (Poetry)
SECRETS AND LIES (Autobiography Pt.2)
SAD, LONELY AND A LONG WAY FROM HOME
(Autobiography Pt.1)

Under: A.J McGinty

CHASING HORIZONS (Poetry)
ROSIE CHASING RAINBOWS (Children Book)

COMING SOON!

HOUSE OF ANNIE LINN BIRD (Fiction)
(First in a heptalogy series)
SIMPLE FOOD (Cookbook)
(A journey with food after my diagnosis)
RAT INFESTED BRITAIN (Non-Fiction)
THE UNHEARD SCREAMS OF THE ASYLUM (Non-Fiction)

Printed in Great Britain
by Amazon

35727963R00043